FOR SHEET METAL FABRICATORS

9 MONEY DRAINING MISTAKES COSTING YOU CRORES

FOR SHEET METAL FABRICATORS

9 MONEY DRAINING MISTAKES COSTING YOU CRORES

Harsh Ashish

Worldwide Published by
Pendown Press

PENDOWN PRESS LLP

An ISO 9001 & ISO 14001 Certified Co.,

Regd. Office: 3767A, Kanhaiya Nagar,

Tri Nagar, Delhi-110035

Ph.: 8130886000, 9650072927, 8595249536

E-mail: info@pendownpress.com

Branch Office: 1A/2A, 20, Hari Sadan, Ansari Road,

Daryaganj, New Delhi-110002

Ph.: 011-45794768

Website: PendownPress.com

Edition: 2024

Price: ₹ 399/-

ISBN: 978-93-5554-847-4

Layout and Cover Designed by Pendown Graphics Team
Printed and Bound in India by Thomson Press India Ltd.

CONTENTS

Dedication

I dedicate this book with great respect
to the hardworking sheet metal fabrication
businesses of India.

Your dedication, sweat, and labor often go unnoticed,
as you tirelessly bend and cut metal day and night
to build our nation's infrastructure.

You are the backbone of India's industrial sector,
playing a crucial role in its economic development.
My salute to all of you.

With endless love and gratitude,

Harsh Ashish

Acknowledgements

I want to thank all the sheet metal shops that helped me write this book to support the industry. Many shop owners took time from their busy schedules to provide valuable insights and feedback on manufacturing best practices.

Their expert knowledge, learned in the factory trenches, forms the basis of recommendations I am offering. Without these shops generously sharing details about their obstacles, successes, and machines, I could not have produced this useful guide.

My deepest thanks to all.

❖   ❖   ❖   ❖

Introduction

Running a sheet metal fabrication shop requires a lot of money. The machines are very expensive to buy, and the prices of raw materials go up and down. Workers need be trained to use the complicated machines, and special tools wear out quickly, so they must be replaced often. All of these costs make it hard to make enough profit. It is a risky business that needs a lot of cash to operate.

Managing a sheet metal fabrication company takes strong nerves because there's a lot of uncertainty and pressure involved. From dealing with unpredictable market changes to ensuring smooth operations despite technical challenges, it's a demanding job.

Yet, despite these challenges, there's a spirit of resilience among those in the industry. It's a testament to their determination and willingness to overcome obstacles.

I salute you for your hard work and dedication.

But what if I told you there's a solution to these problems?

It's a method learned through experience, designed to help alleviate the financial burdens of running a sheet metal fabrication shop.

TRUST ME, I SPEAK WITH MY EXPEREINCE.

❖   ❖   ❖   ❖

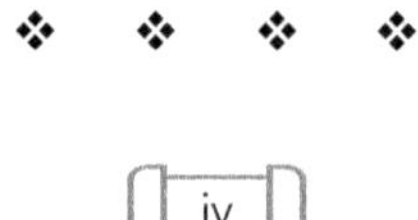

Hello, my name is Harsh Ashish. I am a CNC Punching and Press Brake tooling specialist. My journey into manufacturing precision toolings began seven years ago, early in my career.

As these years passed, three things happened to me: -

1. My knowledge in this industry grew to a great extent.
2. My business expanded exponentially, with impressive gains annually
3. I discovered my true calling - a purpose I am passionately and emotionally aligned with.

I realized that "manufacturing" world-class sheet metal fabrication tooling is not my purpose of life. Simply fulfilling tooling orders as a transactional relationship did not bring me joy.

It took me time to realize that educating and creating awareness for sheet metal businesses is where my true passion lies. This became my life's purpose, and this book marks my first step in that direction.

I travelled to various cities, and did deep discussions with hundreds of sheet metal businesses and tried to understand their pain points, where they face challenges, and what causes loss in terms of money and productivity.

Carefully documenting these discussions, I created a database of issues and solved them one by one. Now, I am ready to present to you these problems and their solutions in a simple and understandable manner.

You may wonder - why am I giving away such useful information for free?

Firstly, my purpose is not monetary gain, but rather to help businesses like yours increase profits. By sharing powerful ideas, we all rise together.

Second, due to time constraints, I am unable to coach everyone personally. Thus, this book serves as my heartfelt gift to sheet metal fabrication businesses, with no expectation of anything in return.

The knowledge within these pages is invaluable. I have spent many years working hard to develop these methods and could have monetized this advice, but I believe true wealth is in improving lives.

I hope these lessons will guide you towards the path of success in the field of sheet metal fabrication. So, without further ado, let's explore these nine lessons I've learned and now I want you to share with you.

Let's GO...

Your trusted tooling expert,

- Harsh Ashish

PS- Throughout the book, I will be discussing about various downloadable files.

I know that you will be tempted to skip the lessons and directly jump and download them, I advise you to first read and understand the lessons discussed. These files are made for you and will remain accessible for your benefit. That's my promise.

Machine Maintainance
The Most Ignored Part

Through my extensive experience, I've witnessed companies investing in premium tooling from leading manufacturers worldwide, but sadly, their CNC punch press and press brake machines are often in poor condition. It's crucial for organizations to recognize that machines and tooling go hand in hand for optimal performance. Even with the best tools, if maintenance is ignored, it can seriously weaken their effectiveness.

Understanding Why it Matters

Taking care of machines isn't just a boring job—it's super important. Just like a finely tuned musical instrument sounds great, a well-kept machine works perfectly. If we don't take care of our machines, they can start having problems like not working right or breaking down often.

Not keeping our machines in good shape can cause lots of problems. When a machine breaks down unexpectedly, we can't finish making things on time, which can make customers unhappy. Plus, fixing broken machines costs a lot of money and can make it hard for a business to grow.

What We Can Do About It ?

The good news is, we can do things to prevent these problems. We can make a plan to regularly check and fix our machines so they stay in good condition. We can also make sure someone is responsible for doing this and that everyone knows what needs to be done and when.

Making Sure Everyone's on Board

It's important for everyone in the team to understand how important it is to take care of the machines. We can keep track of what's been done and who's responsible for it. And we can teach everyone how to do basic maintenance tasks so we can all help keep things running smoothly.

Why it Matters in the Long Run

Taking care of our machines might seem like a hassle, but it's worth it. It helps us avoid big problems later on and keeps everything running smoothly. So, even though it might not seem like the most exciting part of the job, it's definitely one of the most important.

"Machine Maintainance Is Important"

Some of you might say that we take adequate care of our machines. However, it's essential to pause and reflect—are you really giving your machines the attention they require?

Do you have a dedicated resource only to do machine maintenance?

And if you do, is there a structured plan outlining which parts need to be checked or cleaned and when?

If these questions give you pause for thought, fear not. I've prepared a detailed checklist for machine maintenance. This will help you remember what needs to be done and when. There are tasks to do every day, week, month, every six months, and every year.

Simply print out this checklist and affix it somewhere visible on your machine, ensuring that everyone in your workshop can access and adhere to it diligently.

❖   ❖   ❖   ❖

Tool Inventory

The Game Changer

Managing tools is like playing a strategic game in the sheet metal business, and having control over your tool inventory can be a game changer. As you work in this industry, you accumulate a variety of tools over the years—some essential for regular tasks, others only used occasionally. But without proper management, this inventory can become a chaotic mess, leading to financial losses.

Imagine this: You're in the middle of a project, and you realize you're missing a crucial tool. It's frustrating, time-consuming, and can even result in delays or errors in your work. That's why effective tool inventory management is essential.

Now, you might think, "Can't I just use some off-the-shelf software to manage my tool inventory?" Well, the reality is, finding a ready-made solution that perfectly fits your needs can be challenging. So, I took it upon myself to address this problem.

I developed a tool inventory management software designed specifically for the sheet metal industry. This software is a game changer—it allows you to keep track of every tool in your inventory with ease. Whether it's alerting you when a tool is running low or providing insights into excess stock, this software puts you in control.

But perhaps the most exciting feature is its ability to calculate the total cost of your tooling inventory. Knowing the value of your tools gives you a better understanding of your investments and helps you make informed decisions about your resources.

With this tool inventory management software, you can level up your game in the sheet metal business. You'll spend less time searching for tools and more time focusing on what really matters—producing high-quality work efficiently and effectively.

And here's the best part, I've developed this tooling software in the form of a sheet that can be stored in your Google Drive, allowing multiple users to work on it simultaneously. This makes collaboration seamless and ensures that everyone on your team has access to the latest tool inventory information.

This is how the tooling software looks.

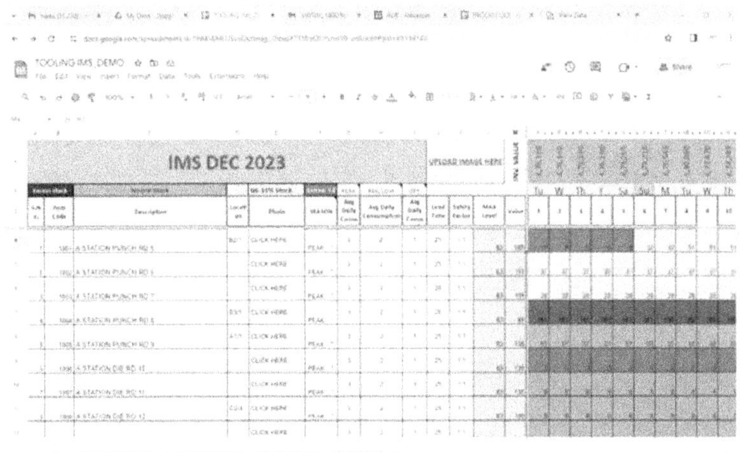

Tool Maintainance

Seldom Done

Over my many years of experience, I've consistently observed a pattern: when tools are purchased, they often come with a hefty price tag and high expectations. However, once these tools find their way to the shop floor, they tend to receive inadequate attention. In the bustling world of sheet metal fabrication, where meeting deadlines and maintaining productivity are top priorities, the maintenance of tools is frequently overlooked. Nevertheless, neglecting this crucial aspect can result in dire consequences, ranging from decreased performance to the need for expensive repairs or replacements.

Understanding the Importance

Tools serve as the backbone of any sheet metal operation, facilitating precise cuts, bends, and formations. However, similar to any machinery, they necessitate regular maintenance to operate at their best. Unfortunately, they are often not organized properly, left without any anti-rust treatment, and neglected in various other ways. Without adequate care, tools can deteriorate, becoming dull, misaligned, or damaged, ultimately resulting in subpar outcomes and posing potential safety risks.

Despite its importance, tool maintenance is often overlooked due to time constraints, lack of awareness, or simply a focus on immediate production needs. In many workshops, tools are only serviced when they malfunction, rather than proactively maintained to prevent issues.

Breaking the Cycle

It's important to acknowledge that tooling is an expensive affair, and proper care can save you lacs and lacs of rupees. It's time to break the cycle of neglect and prioritize tool maintenance. Establishing a routine maintenance schedule ensures that tools are regularly inspected, cleaned, and serviced. This proactive approach not only prolongs the lifespan of tools but also enhances their performance and reliability.

Investing in Education

Empowering employees with the knowledge and skills to perform basic tool maintenance is essential. Training sessions or resources on proper cleaning techniques, sharpening procedures, and alignment adjustments equip workers to take ownership of tool maintenance and contribute to the overall efficiency of the operation.

Utilizing Technology

Advancements in technology have made tool maintenance more accessible than ever. From automated sharpening systems to digital calibration tools, there are various resources available to streamline maintenance tasks and ensure consistent quality.

While tool maintenance may seem like a time-consuming task, its long-term benefits far outweigh the short-term inconvenience. By investing time and effort into maintaining tools, sheet metal fabricators can improve efficiency, reduce costs, and ultimately, deliver higher quality products. It's time to shift the mindset from "fixing when broken" to "maintaining for success" in the sheet metal industry.

As I have previously emphasized the importance of machine maintenance, tooling maintenance has equal importance. And for this, I have prepared a comprehensive tooling maintenance manual. Within this manual, you will find various methods to maintain your tooling effectively, ensuring they provide optimal performance throughout their service life.

Tool Re-Grinding

*The Thing No One Wants
To Do In Shop Floor*

Tool re-grinding often gets overlooked in many shop floors. From my experience, I've noticed that this important task is often forgotten about amidst the hustle and bustle of daily operations. In a survey I conducted, it became clear that untrained operators are usually responsible for tool re-grinding, which can lead to problems and money lost. Ignoring this vital aspect of tool maintenance can result in decreased productivity and increased costs in the long run.

Understanding Tool Value

It's important to realize that every millimeter of a tool is valuable. If too much material is removed during re-grinding, it means losing a lot of money. While buying expensive tool grinders might seem like a solution, it's more about how well the operator can use them. Proper training and attention to detail can make a significant difference in maximizing the lifespan and effectiveness of tools, ultimately saving valuable resources for the shop floor.

Maximizing Tool Grinders

Using tool grinders efficiently is key to saving money and making the most of resources. While fancy machines can help, it's really about how skilled the person using them is. Sometimes, simple surface grinders are used really well, showing that proper training and using available tools wisely are crucial. By investing in training programs and empowering operators with the knowledge to utilize tool grinders effectively, shop floors can enhance productivity and minimize wastage.

Train Your Team

Training your team in tool grinding is essential for saving money and working better. My team of experts is here to provide customized training right in your shop. With the right skills and knowledge, your team can grind tools better, saving resources and boosting productivity. By prioritizing training initiatives and emphasizing the importance of tool re-grinding, shop floors can achieve greater efficiency and success in their operations, ultimately driving growth and profitability in the competitive marketplace.

Data Safety

What is That?

Imagine one day you find that all your important drawings and NC programmes get deleted from the computer, with no way to recover them. It's a terrifying thought, isn't it?

There are countless ways this nightmare scenario could unfold:

1. Your employee deleted the data "by mistake".
2. Some outgoing employee took a grudge on you and deleted the whole data.
3. Your computer got crashed unexpectedly.
4. Or perhaps, it's just a stroke of bad luck.

To counter this critical issue, I set out on a mission to discover a secure and reliable method for storing your vital data.

Now, I want you to explore the world of Google Drive. With Google Drive, you can securely store thousands of files, knowing that your data is in the safe hands of Google. Additionally, Google Drive offers features such as automatic backup and version history, providing an added layer of protection against data loss

I have prepared some instructional videos to guide you through the process of setting up and utilizing Google Drive effectively. These videos will not only help you safeguard your data but also ensure that you can access it from anywhere, at any time, giving you peace of mind and greater flexibility in managing your important files.

Diverse Tooling Systems

Causes Confusion

The realm of tooling systems is vast and varied, presenting a multitude of options and configurations that can often lead to confusion and uncertainty. With so many different types of tools available, each having its own set of features and benefits, it's no wonder that navigating this landscape can be challenging for businesses.

Understanding the Complexity

The complexity of diverse tooling systems stems from the wide range of industries and applications they serve. From CNC punching to press brake operations, each sector has its own unique requirements and specifications, resulting in a diverse array of tooling solutions.

Challenges Faced

One major challenge with diverse tooling systems is the overwhelming number of options available. With numerous manufacturers offering a variety of tools, choosing the right system for your needs can be daunting.

Over time, we've observed various tooling manufacturers developing their unique styles. However, a significant drawback is the lack of compatibility between tools from different manufacturers. This often forces users to stick to one manufacturer's tooling style. If they need to switch tooling for any reason, they must change their entire tooling setup, adding further complexity to the process.

Also, having multiple tooling style creates a lot of confusion at the time of ordering tools, isn't it??

Standardize the Tooling Style

My advice is to standardize the tooling style within your company. By adopting one tooling style exclusively, you streamline operations and minimize compatibility issues. This approach ensures uniformity across your tooling inventory and simplifies maintenance and replacement processes. Additionally, it fosters consistency in production workflows, enhancing efficiency and productivity. So, make it a rule: one company, one tooling style. Period.

Coating

Really Required?

Coating technology has undoubtedly been a game-changer, solving many problems across different industries for the past years and I have no doubt in my mind about it. It's an incredible invention that has transformed the way we protect and enhance materials. But let's take a closer look at how coating fits into our industry.

In our line of work, coating can make a big difference, but it comes with its own set of considerations. While it's great for solving certain problems, it's essential to think carefully about whether it's truly necessary for what we're doing. Buying tools with coating can be a pricey affair and add a significant chunk to our project costs. So, before we jump into investing in coated tools, let's pause and consider whether they're absolutely essential for our needs.

Now, don't get me wrong—coated tools are fantastic. They can really boost performance and durability. However, it's worth giving uncoated tools a chance first. You might be surprised at how well they can do the job. And if you find down the line that you do need coating, you can always get it done by your tooling supplier as needed.

But here's something else to consider: while coating can offer benefits like increased durability and protection, it's not always the only solution. Sometimes, simple maintenance and proper handling of tools can go a long way in ensuring their longevity and performance. So, before jumping to the conclusion that coating is the answer, let's explore all our options and make informed decisions based on our specific needs and circumstances.

By taking this approach, we can potentially save a lot of money while still achieving the results we need. It's all about finding the balance between performance and cost-effectiveness in our industry.

Tool Trials

Do it Carefully

Congratulations on acquiring your new, valuable forming tool! This addition is sure to enhance the quality of your final product. However, as the tool arrived, your operator conducted a trial and BANG!!! He broke the tool on his first attempt.

It's a scenario I've witnessed all too often in my years of experience: the tool arrives, the operator conducts a trial, and suddenly, disaster strikes—the tool breaks on the very first attempt. And trust me, in 90% of the cases, the operator is not at fault.

The root cause often lies with the tooling company failing to provide a comprehensive tooling setup instruction sheet or manual. Without proper guidance, operators and programmers are left in the dark about the intricacies of the tool's operation.

To avoid such mishaps in the future, make it a standard practice to request a tooling setup sheet or manual from your tooling supplier whenever ordering a forming tool. These instructions provide invaluable insights into the tool's setup and operation, enabling your team to approach trials with confidence and competence. By familiarizing themselves with the instructions outlined in the setup sheet, operators and programmers gain a deeper understanding of the tool's functionality and limitations. This knowledge not only minimizes the risk of tool breakage but also maximizes the tool's potential, ensuring optimal performance and longevity.

So, remember: handle tool trials with care, armed with the guidance provided in the tooling setup sheet. With proper preparation and attention to detail, you can harness the full capabilities of your forming tool and achieve outstanding results in your production processes.

Required - Accurate Hole Sizes

But Not Getting

In various applications, precision is paramount, especially when it comes to creating holes with specific tolerances. Take, for instance, heat exchanger end plates where copper tubes must pass through accurately punched holes. In such scenarios, achieving holes within H7 tolerance is crucial for ensuring proper functionality and performance.

However, despite the importance of precise hole sizes, achieving them can often be challenging. Many manufacturers struggle to consistently produce holes with the required accuracy, leading to inefficiencies and potential issues downstream.

To address this challenge effectively, it's essential to communicate your requirements to the tooling manufacturer when ordering tools. By clearly specifying the need for accurate hole sizes within H7 tolerance, you can ensure that the necessary adjustments are made to the punches and dies to achieve the desired results.

Achieving accurate punched holes on a CNC punching machine requires specific modifications to the tooling. These adjustments are necessary to maintain consistency and precision, even after multiple re-grinds of the punches and dies.

By proactively addressing the need for accurate hole sizes and collaborating closely with your tooling manufacturer, you can minimize discrepancies and ensure that your components meet the required specifications. This proactive approach not only enhances the quality and performance of your products but also contributes to overall efficiency and customer satisfaction.

❖   ❖   ❖   ❖

LET'S RECAP...

So, we have discussed various topics, and let me lay more emphasis on the importance of these lessons.

Rest assured that once you apply your focus on these lessons, you will see remarkable growth and cost-effectiveness in your sheet metal fabrication business.

I understand that these points might feel a little overwhelming at first. My advice to you is not to try to implement all this knowledge in on go.

So, here is a quick summery of what we have learned:

1. **Machine maintenance** must be done using a checklist.
2. Find a way to organise your **tooling inventory.**
3. **Maintaining your tooling** is the most important activity.
4. **Tool re-grinding** is not a part-time activity.
5. **Protect your drawing and NC files** from getting deleted.
6. Do not keep a **bouquet of tooling systems** in your shop floor.
7. Analyse the **need of coating** for your applications.
8. Conduct **tool trials** carefully.
9. For the **need of accurate hole size,** inform your tooling supplier about it.

These lessons, when implemented gradually and systematically, will undoubtedly lead to significant improvements in your operations and outcomes.

Team Training
Take Expert Help

I have observed businesses investing in the latest machinery and getting the most expensive tooling, yet they often overlook the importance of developing the skills of their team who will be using them.

Imagine, if your team is not able to get the most efficiency of the expensive setup you have purchased. It's like money draining out of your system with every passing minute.

Here, I want to emphasize the importance of a team training calendar.

A well-trained team is:

1. Motivated
2. Aligned with your goals
3. Able to make full use of the equipment

You can achieve this by leveraging the knowledge base you've developed with your years of experience, or you can opt to hire an external agency to do that.

Regardless of the approach, investing in team training will elevate your game to the next level.

Conclusion

In this book I could have given more emphasis on each lesson. But I wanted to keep the information short and crisp for your better understanding.

It's like slowly wading into water. First, you dip your toes in to try it out. As you get more comfortable, you take small steps to go deeper. There's no rush. You learn and add bits at your own pace.

I'm in no way saying that implementing all this information is tough, but you will definitely speed up your process with the right guidance.

So, now,

There are two ways to do it -

You and your team can do it on your own. I have tried my best to explain these points in simple manner. A little bit of brainstorming will start giving you results.

Or,

You can take my help. As a leading manufacturer of CNC punch press and press brake tooling, I know the nitty-gritty in great depth, and you can have me by your side. This way, you will speed up your implementation and get to hit the bullseye in one go.

Now time to take action.

As I mentioned at the beginning, all the collateral mentioned in this book is for you to start implementing. But by just giving them to you will not serve the greater purpose.

The files and tools will just simply sit hidden in your computer in some drive.

I want you to scan the QR code now, and I will personally handhold you on a video call to get these tools implemented for you and your

Have an expert by your side.
HAVE US BY YOUR SIDE.

❖   ❖   ❖   ❖